Positive Psychology

Unlock the Power of Positive Thinking and Enhance Your Life with the Proven Techniques of Positive Psychology: A Complete Guide to a Happier, Fulfilling Life

Lance P. Richards

I0620188

Positive Psychology: Unlock the Power of Positive Thinking and Enhance Your Life with the Proven Techniques of Positive Psychology: A Complete Guide to a Happier, Fulfilling Life

Table of Contents

01: Introduction to Positive Psychology

Positive psychology is the scientific study of human strengths, virtues, and optimal functioning. It was founded as a field of study in 1998 by Martin Seligman, who aimed to shift the focus of psychology from solely studying pathology and negative aspects of human behavior, to understanding and promoting well-being and happiness. In the years since its inception, positive psychology has grown into a thriving field with a rich body of research and practical applications for individuals, organizations, and communities.

Positive psychology is concerned with the study of positive emotions, positive experiences, and positive personal characteristics. Positive emotions are the pleasurable, enjoyable feelings that people experience in response to positive events or circumstances. These emotions can range from simple pleasures, like eating a good meal or spending time with friends, to more complex feelings like contentment, satisfaction, and joy. Positive experiences are subjective, and may include things like meaningful work, loving relationships, personal growth, and spiritual experiences. Personal characteristics, also known as strengths and virtues, are traits and behaviors that are associated with well-being and happiness, and can be cultivated and developed through intentional effort.

The goal of positive psychology is not to ignore the negative aspects of life, but rather to understand and promote positive emotions, experiences, and personal characteristics in order to enhance well-being and happiness. Positive psychology recognizes that life is not all sunshine and rainbows, and acknowledges the presence of negativity and suffering. However, it argues that focusing on the positive can lead to greater resilience, greater satisfaction with life, and a more meaningful and fulfilling existence.

One of the core principles of positive psychology is that individuals have the capacity to change and grow, and that well-being and happiness can be cultivated and developed. This perspective is in contrast to more traditional psychological theories, which often emphasize external factors and genetic predispositions as the primary drivers of well-being and happiness. Positive psychology argues that individuals have the ability to shape their own happiness and well-being through intentional effort and the cultivation of positive emotions, experiences, and personal characteristics.

In practice, positive psychology has been applied in a variety of contexts, including education, work, and healthcare. In education, positive psychology has been used to promote well-being and happiness among students and teachers, and to create positive learning environments. In the workplace, positive psychology has been applied to increase job satisfaction, employee engagement, and productivity. In healthcare, positive psychology has been used to promote well-being and happiness, as well as to treat various mental health conditions, such as depression and anxiety.

In conclusion, positive psychology is a growing field of study that offers a new and optimistic perspective on the human experience. By focusing on positive emotions, experiences, and personal characteristics, positive psychology offers individuals the opportunity to cultivate and develop well-being and happiness, and to live a more fulfilling and meaningful life. Whether you are looking to improve your personal life, your work life, or the lives of others, the principles and practices of positive psychology provide a valuable and practical foundation for growth and development.

02: The Science Behind Positive Thinking

Positive thinking has been a popular topic for centuries, with many self-help books and motivational speakers extolling its virtues. However, the scientific study of positive thinking is relatively recent, and has been driven by the growth of the field of positive psychology. In this chapter, we will explore the science behind positive thinking, and look at some of the key findings from research in this area.

Positive thinking is defined as the cognitive process of focusing on positive experiences, thoughts, and emotions, and avoiding negative ones. Positive thinking is not simply ignoring negativity and focusing on positive events, but rather actively constructing a positive interpretation of events and experiences. Positive thinking is associated with a range of benefits, including increased happiness, reduced stress and anxiety, improved physical health, and increased life satisfaction.

One of the key scientific theories underlying positive thinking is the broaden-and-build theory, which was first proposed by Barbara Fredrickson. This theory suggests that positive emotions broaden individuals' perspectives and build their personal resources, leading to greater well-being and resilience. Positive emotions are thought to broaden individuals' cognitive and social perspectives, allowing them to see new opportunities and connections, and to build personal resources such as resilience and creativity.

Research has shown that positive thinking can lead to a range of physiological and psychological benefits. For example, positive thinking has been shown to reduce stress, anxiety, and depression, and to increase life satisfaction and happiness. Positive thinking has also been shown to have a positive impact on physical health, including reducing the risk of cardiovascular disease, boosting the immune system, and reducing inflammation.

One of the key mechanisms underlying the benefits of positive thinking is thought to be the activation of the brain's reward system. Positive emotions and experiences activate the brain's reward system, leading to the release of dopamine and other neurotransmitters that are associated with pleasure, motivation, and satisfaction. Positive thinking is also thought to change the way that individuals process and respond to negative events and experiences, making them more resilient and less vulnerable to stress and anxiety.

In conclusion, positive thinking is a powerful tool that has been shown to have a range of benefits for both mental and physical health. The science behind positive thinking supports the idea that individuals have the capacity to influence their own well-being and happiness through the intentional cultivation of positive emotions and experiences. Whether you are looking to improve your mental or physical health, or simply to live a happier and more fulfilling life, the practice of positive thinking is a valuable tool to have in your arsenal.

03: Understanding Your Thoughts and Emotions

In order to fully reap the benefits of positive thinking and the techniques of positive psychology, it is important to have a deep understanding of your own thoughts and emotions. Our thoughts and emotions play a critical role in shaping our experiences, and can have a powerful impact on our overall well-being and happiness. In this chapter, we will explore the role of thoughts and emotions in shaping our lives, and look at some practical techniques for gaining greater insight into your own thoughts and emotions.

Thoughts and emotions are inextricably linked, and our thoughts can greatly impact the emotions that we experience. Negative thoughts can lead to negative emotions such as anxiety, stress, and depression, while positive thoughts can lead to positive emotions such as happiness, joy, and satisfaction. Our thoughts and emotions can also impact our behavior, shaping the choices we make and the actions we take.

One of the key techniques for gaining insight into your thoughts and emotions is mindfulness. Mindfulness is the practice of paying attention to the present moment, without judgment. Mindfulness has been shown to be an effective tool for reducing stress and anxiety, and improving well-being and happiness. Mindfulness can be practiced through meditation, yoga, or simply by paying attention to your thoughts and emotions as they arise in daily life.

Another powerful technique for gaining insight into your thoughts and emotions is journaling. Journaling allows you to reflect on your experiences, thoughts, and emotions, and to gain a deeper understanding of the patterns and tendencies that shape your life. By writing down your thoughts and emotions on a regular basis, you can gain a clearer understanding of your own thought patterns and emotional responses, and identify areas where you may need to make changes in order to cultivate more positive thoughts and emotions.

Cognitive-behavioral therapy (CBT) is another effective tool for gaining insight into your thoughts and emotions. CBT is a type of therapy that helps individuals to identify and change negative thought patterns and behaviors that contribute to mental health issues such as anxiety and depression. By working with a therapist, individuals can gain a deeper understanding of the relationship between their thoughts, emotions, and behaviors, and learn techniques for changing negative patterns and cultivating positive thoughts and emotions.

In conclusion, understanding your thoughts and emotions is a critical step in the process of unlocking the power of positive thinking and enhancing your life through positive psychology. By gaining insight into your own thoughts and emotions, you can identify areas for improvement and cultivate more positive experiences, thoughts, and emotions. Whether you choose to practice mindfulness, journaling, or seek the help of a therapist, taking control of your thoughts and emotions is a powerful step in the journey towards a happier and more fulfilling life.

04: The Power of Gratitude

Gratitude is a powerful emotion that has been shown to have a significant impact on overall well-being and happiness. Gratitude is defined as the feeling of thankfulness and appreciation for the good things in life. Gratitude is not simply a fleeting emotion, but can be cultivated and sustained through intentional practices, and has been shown to have a range of benefits for both mental and physical health.

One of the key benefits of gratitude is that it can help to shift our focus away from negative experiences and towards the positive aspects of our lives. When we practice gratitude, we become more aware of the good things in our lives, and are less likely to be overwhelmed by the challenges and difficulties that we face. This shift in perspective can have a profound impact on our well-being, helping to reduce stress and anxiety and increase feelings of happiness and contentment.

Gratitude has also been shown to improve physical health. Studies have found that individuals who practice gratitude experience lower levels of stress hormones, and a stronger immune system response. Gratitude has also been linked to better sleep, improved heart health, and a lower risk of depression and anxiety.

In order to cultivate gratitude, it is important to engage in intentional practices that help to increase your awareness of the good things in your life. One effective technique is to keep a gratitude journal, where you write down things that you are thankful for on a daily basis. Another technique is to take time each day to reflect on the good things in your life, and to express your gratitude to others through words or actions. Engaging in acts of kindness and generosity can also help to increase feelings of gratitude, as well as providing a positive impact on those around you.

Gratitude can also be cultivated through mindfulness, which involves paying attention to the present moment and the positive experiences that you are currently enjoying. By focusing your attention on the present moment, you can become more aware of the good things in your life, and experience greater feelings of gratitude.

Finally, it is important to recognize that gratitude is not simply a one-time event, but a practice that requires ongoing effort and commitment. By making gratitude a regular part of your life, you can experience the ongoing benefits that it provides, and cultivate a happier and more fulfilling life.

In conclusion, gratitude is a powerful tool for enhancing well-being and happiness, and has been shown to have a range of positive effects on both mental and physical health. By cultivating gratitude through intentional practices such as journaling, mindfulness, and acts of kindness, you can experience the benefits of a more positive and grateful outlook, and live a happier, more fulfilling life.

05: Cultivating Positive Relation-ships

Positive relationships are an essential component of a happy and fulfilling life. Our relationships with others have a significant impact on our overall well-being, and can greatly contribute to our happiness and contentment. At the same time, negative relationships can be a source of stress, anxiety, and depression. It is therefore essential to cultivate positive relationships in order to enhance our well-being and lead a happier, more fulfilling life.

One of the key benefits of positive relationships is that they provide emotional support and a sense of connection. When we have strong and positive relationships with others, we feel more connected, less isolated, and better equipped to deal with the challenges of life. Positive relationships can also provide a sense of security and stability, helping us to feel more confident and empowered in our daily lives.

Another benefit of positive relationships is that they can provide a source of inspiration and motivation. When we are surrounded by people who encourage and support us, we are more likely to take risks and pursue our goals, leading to a more fulfilling and satisfying life.

05: CULTIVATING POSITIVE RELATIONSHIPS

In order to cultivate positive relationships, it is important to engage in intentional behaviors that promote connection, respect, and understanding. This may include making time for regular social interactions, actively listening to others, and expressing gratitude and appreciation for their positive qualities and actions. Additionally, it is important to avoid negative behaviors that can harm relationships, such as criticism, blame, and gossip.

One effective technique for cultivating positive relationships is to engage in activities that promote mutual interests and shared experiences. This can be as simple as spending time with friends and family, participating in group activities, or volunteering for a cause that is important to you. When we engage in activities that bring us together with others, we are more likely to develop strong and positive relationships, and to experience the benefits that these relationships provide.

It is also important to recognize that positive relationships require effort and commitment from all parties involved. To develop and maintain positive relationships, it is essential to be open and honest, to listen and support others, and to engage in regular communication and interaction. By making positive relationships a priority, and engaging in intentional behaviors that promote connection and understanding, you can experience the benefits of strong and positive relationships, and lead a happier, more fulfilling life.

In conclusion, positive relationships are a critical component of a happy and fulfilling life, providing emotional support, a sense of connection, and a source of inspiration and motivation. By making positive relationships a priority, engaging in intentional behaviors that promote connection and understanding, and avoiding negative behaviors that can harm relationships, you can cultivate strong and positive relationships, and experience the benefits that these relationships provide.

06: Positive Self-Talk and Affirmations

Positive self-talk and affirmations are powerful tools for enhancing well-being and promoting positive thinking. These techniques involve speaking positively to oneself, and using positive statements to reinforce positive beliefs and attitudes. When we engage in positive self-talk and affirmations, we can improve our self-esteem, increase our motivation, and reduce negative emotions such as anxiety and stress.

Positive self-talk involves speaking kindly and respectfully to oneself, just as one would speak to a friend or loved one. This includes avoiding negative self-criticism, and instead focusing on one's strengths and positive qualities. By speaking kindly and respectfully to oneself, we can develop a more positive self-image, and improve our overall well-being.

Affirmations are positive statements that are used to reinforce positive beliefs and attitudes. These statements are designed to counteract negative thoughts and beliefs, and to promote positive thinking. Affirmations can be used to address a wide range of issues, including low self-esteem, stress, anxiety, and negative self-talk.

To use affirmations effectively, it is important to choose statements that resonate with you, and to repeat them regularly. This can be done through writing, speaking, or simply repeating the affirmations to oneself. It is also helpful to use affirmations in a positive and confident tone, and to focus on the present moment rather than the future or past.

In addition to using affirmations, it is important to adopt a positive self-talk style in general. This can involve recognizing and challenging negative self-talk, and instead focusing on positive and constructive self-talk. When we engage in positive self-talk, we can increase our confidence and motivation, and reduce negative emotions such as anxiety and stress.

Another effective technique for promoting positive self-talk is to surround yourself with positive and supportive people. When we are surrounded by positive and supportive individuals, we are more likely to engage in positive self-talk, and to adopt a positive outlook on life. Additionally, engaging in activities that bring joy and fulfillment, such as exercise, meditation, and spending time in nature, can also promote positive self-talk and a positive outlook.

In conclusion, positive self-talk and affirmations are powerful tools for enhancing well-being and promoting positive thinking. By speaking kindly and respectfully to oneself, using positive affirmations, adopting a positive self-talk style, and surrounding oneself with positive and supportive individuals, we can improve our self-esteem, increase our motivation, and reduce negative emotions such as anxiety and stress. By making positive self-talk and affirmations a priority, we can lead a happier, more fulfilling life.

07: Mindfulness and Meditation

Mindfulness and meditation are ancient practices that have been gaining popularity in recent years due to their numerous mental and physical health benefits. These practices involve paying attention to the present moment, and focusing on one's thoughts, feelings, and sensations without judgment. Mindfulness and meditation can help to reduce stress and anxiety, increase feelings of happiness and well-being, and improve overall quality of life.

Mindfulness involves paying attention to the present moment, and being fully present in the moment without distraction. This can be achieved through practices such as paying attention to one's breathing, observing one's thoughts and feelings without judgment, and focusing on the present moment without worrying about the future or dwelling on the past. When we practice mindfulness, we can improve our ability to regulate our emotions, increase our mental clarity, and reduce stress and anxiety.

Meditation is a mindfulness-based practice that involves focusing on a specific object, thought, or activity to calm the mind and improve overall well-being. There are many different types of meditation, including mindfulness meditation, loving-kindness meditation, and visualization meditation. When we meditate, we can increase our self-awareness, improve our ability to focus, and reduce negative thoughts and emotions.

One of the key benefits of mindfulness and meditation is that they can help to reduce stress and anxiety. When we practice mindfulness and meditation regularly, we can develop the ability to stay calm and centered, even in the face of stress and anxiety. Additionally, mindfulness and meditation can help to improve sleep quality, increase feelings of happiness and well-being, and reduce symptoms of depression.

Another benefit of mindfulness and meditation is that they can help to improve physical health. These practices have been shown to reduce inflammation, improve immune function, and lower blood pressure. Additionally, mindfulness and meditation can also improve physical conditions such as chronic pain and cardiovascular disease.

To get the most out of mindfulness and meditation, it is important to practice regularly and consistently. This can involve setting aside time each day to meditate, or incorporating mindfulness practices into everyday activities. It is also important to approach mindfulness and meditation with an open mind, and to be patient and persistent in the face of challenges.

In conclusion, mindfulness and meditation are powerful tools for improving mental and physical health. By paying attention to the present moment, and focusing on our thoughts and feelings without judgment, we can reduce stress and anxiety, increase feelings of happiness and well-being, and improve overall quality of life. By making mind-fulness and meditation a regular part of our lives, we can tap into the power of positive thinking, and lead a happier, more fulfilling life.

08: The Benefits of Positive Thinking

Positive thinking is a powerful tool for improving our mental and emotional well-being. It involves focusing on the positive aspects of our lives, and approaching challenges and difficulties with a hopeful and optimistic attitude. Positive thinking has been shown to have a wide range of benefits, including increased happiness, reduced stress and anxiety, and improved physical health.

One of the key benefits of positive thinking is that it can help to increase feelings of happiness and well-being. When we focus on the positive aspects of our lives, we are more likely to feel satisfied and content, and less likely to experience negative emotions such as anger, sadness, and frustration. Additionally, positive thinking can help to increase resilience, and improve our ability to cope with challenges and difficulties.

Another benefit of positive thinking is that it can help to reduce stress and anxiety. When we approach challenges and difficulties with a positive attitude, we are less likely to feel overwhelmed and stressed, and more likely to find creative and effective solutions. Additionally, positive thinking can help to improve our overall mental health, and reduce symptoms of depression and anxiety.

Positive thinking can also have a positive impact on our physical health. Research has shown that positive thinking can help to reduce inflammation, improve immune function, and lower blood pressure. Additionally, positive thinking can improve physical conditions such as chronic pain and cardiovascular disease.

To develop a positive thinking mindset, it is important to focus on the positive aspects of our lives, and to cultivate gratitude and appreciation. This can involve setting aside time each day to reflect on the things that we are grateful for, and to focus on our strengths and positive attributes. Additionally, it is important to challenge negative thoughts and replace them with positive affirmations.

In conclusion, positive thinking is a powerful tool for improving mental and physical health. By focusing on the positive aspects of our lives, and approaching challenges and difficulties with a hopeful and optimistic attitude, we can increase feelings of happiness and well-being, reduce stress and anxiety, and improve overall quality of life. By making positive thinking a regular part of our lives, we can tap into the power of positive psychology, and lead a happier, more fulfilling life.

09: Overcoming Negative Thoughts and Emotions

Negative thoughts and emotions can be a challenge to overcome, but they are an important part of our lives that can teach us valuable lessons. However, if negative thoughts and emotions become too frequent or intense, they can start to affect our mental and emotional well-being, leading to feelings of stress, anxiety, and depression.

One of the key strategies for overcoming negative thoughts and emotions is to practice mindfulness and meditation. Mindfulness involves paying attention to the present moment, and focusing on our thoughts and feelings without judgment. When we practice mindfulness, we can improve our ability to regulate our emotions, and reduce the frequency and intensity of negative thoughts and emotions.

Another strategy for overcoming negative thoughts and emotions is to engage in positive self-talk and affirmations. Positive self-talk involves speaking to ourselves in a supportive and encouraging manner, and focusing on our strengths and positive attributes. Positive affirmations involve repeating positive statements to ourselves, such as "I am worthy and deserving of love and happiness." By engaging in positive self-talk and affirmations, we can counter-act negative thoughts and emotions, and improve our over-all mental and emotional well-being.

Additionally, it is important to identify and challenge negat-ive thought patterns and beliefs. Negative thoughts and emotions often stem from unhelpful beliefs that we hold about ourselves, such as "I am not good enough" or "I can never be happy." By identifying these beliefs and challen-ging them with evidence and alternative perspectives, we can reduce their impact on our lives.

Finally, it is important to cultivate positive relationships and social support. Positive relationships with friends, fam-ily, and loved ones can help to provide us with a source of comfort and support, and can help us to overcome negative thoughts and emotions. Additionally, participating in com-munity activities and engaging in hobbies and interests that we enjoy can also help to improve our mental and emo-tional well-being.

In conclusion, negative thoughts and emotions are a normal part of life, but they can become overwhelming if they be-come too frequent or intense. By practicing mindfulness and meditation, engaging in positive self-talk and affirmations, challenging negative thought patterns and beliefs, and cultivating positive relationships and social support, we can overcome negative thoughts and emotions, and improve our overall mental and emotional well-being.

10: Setting and Achieving Positive Goals

Setting and achieving positive goals is a crucial aspect of positive psychology, as it provides a sense of purpose, direction, and fulfillment in life. Positive goals are those that align with our values, interests, and strengths, and that help to enhance our overall well-being.

The first step in setting and achieving positive goals is to identify what is important to us. This can involve reflecting on our values, interests, and strengths, and considering what we want to achieve in different areas of our lives, such as our careers, relationships, and personal growth.

Once we have identified our goals, it is important to set specific, measurable, and achievable goals. Specific goals are those that are clearly defined, such as "I want to get a promotion at work." Measurable goals are those that can be tracked and quantified, such as "I want to read 30 books this year." Achievable goals are those that are realistic and attainable, given our resources and abilities.

Next, it is important to create a plan for achieving our goals. This can involve breaking down larger goals into smaller, manageable tasks, setting deadlines for completing each task, and monitoring our progress along the way. Having a plan helps us to stay focused and motivated, and to overcome any obstacles that may arise.

In order to achieve our goals, it is important to cultivate a positive attitude and a growth mindset. A positive attitude involves focusing on the benefits and opportunities that come with reaching our goals, and approaching challenges and obstacles with a solution-focused mindset. A growth mindset involves embracing challenges and setbacks as opportunities for growth and learning, and recognizing that our abilities and skills can be developed and improved over time.

Finally, it is important to cultivate a support system and seek help when needed. This can involve enlisting the support of friends, family, and loved ones, and seeking guidance and mentorship from experienced individuals in our areas of interest. Having a support system can help us to stay motivated and accountable, and to overcome any obstacles that may arise.

In conclusion, setting and achieving positive goals is a crucial aspect of positive psychology, and can help us to enhance our overall well-being. By identifying our goals, setting specific, measurable, and achievable goals, creating a plan for achieving our goals, cultivating a positive attitude and a growth mindset, and cultivating a support system, we can increase our chances of success, and live a happier, fulfilling life.

11: Strengthening Resilience

Resilience is the ability to bounce back from adversity and to cope effectively with stress and challenges. It is a crucial aspect of positive psychology, as it helps us to maintain our well-being and happiness in the face of life's difficulties.

The first step in strengthening resilience is to understand our personal stressors and triggers. This can involve reflecting on past experiences and identifying what has caused us stress in the past, and what has helped us to cope effectively. It can also involve learning to recognize early warning signs of stress, such as physical symptoms, negative thoughts, and behavioral changes.

Next, it is important to develop healthy coping strategies. This can involve finding healthy ways to manage stress, such as exercise, mindfulness, and relaxation techniques. It can also involve seeking support from friends, family, or mental health professionals, when needed. Having healthy coping strategies helps us to effectively manage stress and adversity, and to maintain our well-being and happiness.

In addition, it is important to cultivate a positive attitude and a growth mindset. A positive attitude involves focusing on the benefits and opportunities that come with adversity, and approaching challenges and obstacles with a solution-focused mindset. A growth mindset involves embracing challenges and setbacks as opportunities for growth and learning, and recognizing that our abilities and skills can be developed and improved over time.

It is also important to build resilience through intentional activities and experiences. This can involve engaging in activities that help us to develop a sense of mastery and control, such as learning a new skill or taking on new challenges. It can also involve exposing ourselves to new experiences and situations, and developing a sense of flexibility and adaptability.

Finally, it is important to cultivate gratitude and maintain a positive outlook on life. Gratitude involves recognizing and appreciating the good things in our lives, and can help us to maintain a positive outlook, even in the face of adversity. A positive outlook involves focusing on the positive aspects of life, and approaching challenges and obstacles with a sense of hope and optimism.

In conclusion, strengthening resilience is a crucial aspect of positive psychology, and can help us to maintain our well-being and happiness in the face of life's difficulties. By understanding our personal stressors and triggers, developing healthy coping strategies, cultivating a positive attitude and a growth mindset, building resilience through intentional activities and experiences, and cultivating gratitude and maintaining a positive outlook, we can increase our resilience and bounce back from adversity with ease.

12: The Impact of Positive Thinking on Physical Health

The relationship between positive thinking and physical health is well established. Positive thinking has been shown to have a number of benefits for physical health, including improved immune function, reduced stress, and better cardiovascular health.

One of the key ways that positive thinking affects physical health is through its impact on stress. Positive thinking has been shown to reduce stress levels, which can help to lower blood pressure and improve heart health. It can also boost the immune system, helping the body to fight off illness and disease more effectively.

Another way that positive thinking affects physical health is through its impact on behavior. Positive thinking has been shown to encourage healthy behaviors, such as regular exercise and healthy eating habits. This, in turn, can improve physical health, as exercise and healthy eating have numerous benefits for the body, including reducing the risk of heart disease, obesity, and other health conditions.

Positive thinking can also impact physical health through its impact on sleep. Positive thinking has been shown to improve sleep quality and reduce the likelihood of sleep disturbances. This is because positive thinking can help to reduce stress and anxiety, which can interfere with sleep.

In addition, positive thinking can also have a positive impact on mental health, which, in turn, can impact physical health. For example, positive thinking has been shown to reduce symptoms of depression and anxiety, which can help to reduce stress and improve overall health.

It is important to note that while positive thinking can have numerous benefits for physical health, it is not a substitute for medical treatment. If you are experiencing physical health problems, it is important to seek the advice of a healthcare professional.

In conclusion, positive thinking has a number of benefits for physical health, including improved immune function, reduced stress, better cardiovascular health, healthier behaviors, improved sleep quality, and a positive impact on mental health. By incorporating positive thinking into our daily lives, we can improve our physical health and enhance our overall well-being.

13: Finding Purpose and Meaning in Life

Purpose and meaning in life are important components of overall well-being and happiness. People who have a strong sense of purpose and meaning in life tend to be more satisfied with their lives and are less likely to experience depression and anxiety.

So, what exactly is purpose and meaning in life, and how can it be cultivated? Purpose refers to the reasons or goals that drive a person's behavior and give their life direction. Meaning refers to the sense of significance that a person derives from their experiences and relationships.

Finding purpose and meaning in life can be a lifelong journey, and there is no one right way to do it. However, there are some strategies that can be helpful in the pursuit of purpose and meaning.

One way to find purpose and meaning is to identify your values and passions. This can be done by reflecting on what is important to you and what brings you joy and fulfillment. Once you have identified your values and passions, you can look for ways to incorporate them into your daily life and make them a priority.

Another way to find purpose and meaning is to connect with others and build meaningful relationships. Relationships with family, friends, and community can provide a sense of belonging and give us a sense of purpose and meaning.

Volunteering and contributing to others in your community can also help you find purpose and meaning. By helping others and making a positive impact in the world, you can feel a sense of satisfaction and fulfillment that goes beyond personal gain.

It is also important to set and achieve goals in order to find purpose and meaning in life. Whether it is a personal goal or a goal related to your values and passions, setting and achieving goals can give you a sense of direction and help you feel like you are making progress in your life.

Finally, it is important to be open to new experiences and challenges. Embracing new challenges and experiences can help you grow as a person and deepen your sense of purpose and meaning.

13: FINDING PURPOSE AND MEANING IN LIFE

In conclusion, finding purpose and meaning in life is an important aspect of overall well-being and happiness. By identifying your values and passions, building meaningful relationships, volunteering and contributing to your community, setting and achieving goals, and being open to new experiences and challenges, you can deepen your sense of purpose and meaning in life.

14: Embracing Positive Emotions

Positive emotions play a crucial role in our overall well-being and happiness. Positive emotions broaden our perspective, foster creativity, and help us build resilience. They also have a positive impact on our relationships and can help us feel more connected to others.

So, what exactly are positive emotions, and how can we cultivate them? Positive emotions include feelings such as joy, love, gratitude, and contentment. These emotions can be experienced in response to positive events and experiences, such as spending time with loved ones, accomplishing a goal, or simply enjoying a beautiful day.

Cultivating positive emotions can be done in a number of ways. One effective strategy is to practice gratitude. Gratitude involves recognizing and appreciating the good things in your life, no matter how small they may be. Practicing gratitude can help you shift your focus away from negative thoughts and emotions, and instead, help you feel more positive and content.

Another strategy for cultivating positive emotions is to engage in activities that bring you joy and fulfillment. This could be anything from playing a musical instrument to hiking in nature. Engaging in activities that you enjoy can help you feel more positive and increase your overall well-being.

In addition to engaging in activities that bring you joy, it is also important to surround yourself with positive people. People who are positive and supportive can help you feel more positive, and can also help you build resilience.

It is also important to recognize and accept your emotions, both positive and negative. By accepting your emotions and allowing yourself to experience them fully, you can learn to manage them in a healthier way and increase your overall well-being.

In conclusion, embracing positive emotions is an important aspect of overall well-being and happiness. By practicing gratitude, engaging in activities that bring you joy and fulfillment, surrounding yourself with positive people, and recognizing and accepting your emotions, you can cultivate positive emotions and experience greater happiness and contentment in life.

15: Building a Positive Work Environment

The workplace is a crucial part of our daily lives, and can have a significant impact on our overall well-being and happiness. A positive work environment can increase job satisfaction, improve productivity, and foster a sense of belonging and fulfillment. On the other hand, a negative work environment can lead to stress, burnout, and decreased job satisfaction.

So, how can we create a positive work environment? There are several strategies that can help. One of the most important is to promote open and effective communication. Encouraging open communication between colleagues, supervisors, and subordinates can help foster a sense of trust and understanding, and can lead to more effective collaboration and problem-solving.

Another important aspect of building a positive work environment is to provide opportunities for personal and professional growth. Providing training and development opportunities, such as workshops, conferences, and mentorship programs, can help employees feel valued and empowered, and can also help to retain top talent.

15: BUILDING A POSITIVE WORK ENVIRONMENT

It is also important to create a supportive and inclusive work culture. This can be done by promoting diversity and inclusivity, encouraging a healthy work-life balance, and promoting a positive work-life integration.

In addition to these strategies, it is also important to recognize and reward positive behaviors and accomplishments. This can help to build a positive and supportive workplace culture, and can also help to motivate and engage employees.

Another crucial aspect of building a positive work environment is to address any negative factors that may be impacting the workplace. This could include workplace stress, toxic workplace dynamics, or workplace bullying. Addressing these negative factors can help to create a more positive and supportive work environment, and can also help to improve the overall well-being and happiness of employees.

In conclusion, building a positive work environment is an important aspect of overall well-being and happiness. By promoting open and effective communication, providing opportunities for personal and professional growth, creating a supportive and inclusive work culture, recognizing and rewarding positive behaviors and accomplishments, and addressing negative factors in the workplace, you can create a positive work environment that can lead to greater job satisfaction, productivity, and overall well-being.

16: Enhancing Creativity with Positive Thinking

Creativity is a crucial aspect of our lives, and plays a vital role in personal and professional success. Whether we are creating art, writing music, or developing innovative solutions to complex problems, creativity is essential to our growth and development.

Positive thinking can play a significant role in enhancing our creativity. When we adopt a positive mindset, we become more open to new ideas and experiences, and are more likely to see challenges as opportunities for growth and learning. Additionally, positive thinking can help us to overcome obstacles and barriers, and can provide us with the motivation and confidence we need to pursue our creative goals.

One of the most effective ways to enhance creativity through positive thinking is to practice gratitude. Expressing gratitude can help us to focus on the good in our lives, and can help to improve our overall well-being and happiness. When we are grateful, we are more likely to be open to new experiences and opportunities, and are more likely to see challenges as opportunities for growth and learning.

16: ENHANCING CREATIVITY WITH POSITIVE THINK-ING

Another effective strategy for enhancing creativity with positive thinking is to embrace a growth mindset. A growth mindset involves adopting the belief that our abilities and skills can be developed and improved through effort and perseverance. When we embrace a growth mindset, we are more likely to take risks and pursue our creative goals, even when we face challenges or obstacles.

In addition to these strategies, it is also important to cultivate a positive work environment that supports creativity. This could include providing opportunities for creative expression, encouraging collaboration and teamwork, and promoting a positive and supportive workplace culture.

Finally, it is also important to prioritize self-care and self-compassion. When we are kind and compassionate to ourselves, we are more likely to be open to new experiences and opportunities, and are more likely to pursue our creative goals with confidence and resilience.

In conclusion, positive thinking can play a crucial role in enhancing creativity. By practicing gratitude, embracing a growth mindset, cultivating a positive work environment, and prioritizing self-care and self-compassion, we can enhance our creativity and pursue our creative goals with greater confidence and resilience.

17: The Link between Positive Thinking and Success

Success is a complex concept that means different things to different people. For some, success may be measured by financial wealth, while for others it may be measured by personal fulfillment and happiness. Regardless of how it is defined, success is something that most of us aspire to achieve in our lives.

Positive thinking has been shown to play a significant role in helping individuals achieve success. By adopting a positive mindset, we are more likely to see challenges as opportunities for growth and learning, and are more likely to pursue our goals with confidence and determination. Additionally, positive thinking can help us to overcome obstacles and barriers, and can provide us with the motivation and resilience we need to achieve success.

One of the key benefits of positive thinking is that it helps us to develop a growth mindset. A growth mindset involves adopting the belief that our abilities and skills can be developed and improved through effort and perseverance. When we embrace a growth mindset, we are more likely to take risks and pursue our goals, even when we face challenges or obstacles.

Another way in which positive thinking can contribute to success is by helping us to build positive relationships. Positive relationships provide us with the support and encouragement we need to pursue our goals and overcome obstacles. Additionally, positive relationships can help us to develop new skills and knowledge, and can provide us with opportunities for growth and learning.

Positive thinking can also help us to cultivate resilience, which is an essential ingredient for success. Resilience involves the ability to bounce back from setbacks and challenges, and to persist in the face of obstacles. When we cultivate resilience, we are more likely to pursue our goals with determination, and are more likely to achieve success.

In addition to these benefits, positive thinking can also help us to develop a positive self-image, which is essential for success. A positive self-image involves seeing oneself in a positive light, and believing in one's own abilities and strengths. When we have a positive self-image, we are more likely to pursue our goals with confidence, and are more likely to overcome obstacles and challenges.

17: THE LINK BETWEEN POSITIVE THINKING AND SUCCESS

Finally, it is important to note that success is not just about achieving our goals, but also about enjoying the journey. Positive thinking can help us to savor our experiences, and to find joy and fulfillment in the process of pursuing our goals.

In conclusion, positive thinking can play a crucial role in helping individuals achieve success. By developing a growth mindset, building positive relationships, cultivating resilience, developing a positive self-image, and enjoying the journey, we can increase our chances of achieving success and living a fulfilling life.

18: The Benefits of a Positive Mindset for Children

Positive psychology has shown that cultivating a positive mindset from an early age can have a profound impact on a child's development and well-being. By teaching children to focus on their strengths and to embrace a positive outlook on life, we can help them to build resilience, confidence, and emotional intelligence.

One of the key benefits of a positive mindset for children is that it can help to build resilience. Resilience is the ability to bounce back from setbacks and challenges, and is an essential skill for children to develop as they grow. By teaching children to focus on the positive aspects of their experiences and to adopt a growth mindset, we can help them to build resilience and to better cope with challenges and obstacles.

A positive mindset can also help children to develop confidence and self-esteem. Children who believe in their own abilities and strengths are more likely to take risks and pursue their goals, even when they face challenges or obstacles. Additionally, a positive mindset can help children to develop a positive self-image, which can contribute to their overall sense of well-being and happiness.

18: THE BENEFITS OF A POSITIVE MINDSET FOR CHILDREN

Another important benefit of a positive mindset for children is that it can help to improve their emotional intelligence. Emotional intelligence involves the ability to understand and regulate one's own emotions, as well as the emotions of others. By teaching children to embrace positive emotions and to regulate their negative emotions, we can help them to develop emotional intelligence and to better navigate their social relationships.

In addition to these benefits, a positive mindset can also have a positive impact on children's academic performance. Children who have a positive outlook on life are more likely to be motivated and engaged in their learning, and are more likely to perform well in school. Additionally, a positive mindset can help children to develop a love of learning and to become lifelong learners.

Finally, it is important to note that a positive mindset can also have a positive impact on children's overall well-being and happiness. Children who have a positive outlook on life are more likely to experience happiness and fulfillment, and are less likely to experience stress and anxiety.

In conclusion, cultivating a positive mindset in children can

have a profound impact on their development and well-being. By building resilience, confidence, emotional intelligence, academic performance, and overall well-being, we
can help children to lead happier and more fulfilling lives.

19: Boosting Self-Esteem and Confidence

Self-esteem and confidence are two key components of a positive mindset, and are essential for leading a happy and fulfilling life. Self-esteem refers to our overall evaluation of our worth and abilities, while confidence is the belief in our ability to succeed and achieve our goals.

Unfortunately, many people struggle with low self-esteem and confidence, which can have a negative impact on their lives. Low self-esteem can lead to negative self-talk, anxiety, and depression, while low confidence can make it difficult to pursue our goals and to lead a fulfilling life.

The good news is that there are many techniques and strategies that can help to boost self-esteem and confidence. One of the most effective is the practice of positive self-talk and affirmations. By focusing on our strengths and accomplishments, and by affirming our worth and abilities, we can counteract negative self-talk and build a positive self-image.

Another effective strategy for boosting self-esteem and confidence is setting and achieving positive goals. By setting achievable goals and celebrating our successes, we can build confidence in our abilities and increase our overall sense of self-worth.

In addition to these strategies, mindfulness and meditation can also be helpful for boosting self-esteem and confidence. By helping us to focus on the present moment and to let go of negative thoughts and emotions, mindfulness and meditation can help us to build a positive mindset and to cultivate self-esteem and confidence.

Another important aspect of boosting self-esteem and confidence is cultivating positive relationships. By surrounding ourselves with supportive and encouraging people, we can build a positive support network that can help us to overcome challenges and to build our confidence.

Finally, it is important to embrace positive emotions and to let go of negative emotions. By focusing on joy, gratitude, and other positive emotions, we can build a more positive outlook on life and increase our overall sense of well-being.

In conclusion, there are many strategies and techniques that can help to boost self-esteem and confidence. By focusing on positive self-talk, setting and achieving goals, practicing mindfulness and meditation, cultivating positive relationships, and embracing positive emotions, we can build a more positive mindset and lead a happier and more fulfilling life.

20: Improving Mental Health with Positive Psychology

Mental health is a critical aspect of overall well-being, and can greatly impact our ability to lead a happy and fulfilling life. Positive psychology, with its focus on positive thinking and emotions, can play a key role in improving mental health and promoting well-being.

One of the key ways in which positive psychology can improve mental health is by helping individuals to develop a positive outlook on life. By focusing on positive emotions and experiences, and by reducing the influence of negative thoughts and emotions, positive psychology can help individuals to develop a more positive and optimistic outlook on life.

Another way in which positive psychology can improve mental health is by promoting resilience. Resilience refers to our ability to bounce back from adversity and to maintain well-being in the face of challenges. Positive psychology can help individuals to develop resilience by teaching them coping strategies, such as mindfulness and meditation, that can help them to better manage stress and negative emotions.

In addition to promoting resilience, positive psychology can also help to reduce symptoms of anxiety and depression. By teaching individuals to focus on the present moment, and by encouraging them to let go of negative thoughts and emotions, positive psychology can help to reduce symptoms of anxiety and depression and promote overall well-being.

One of the key ways in which positive psychology can be used to improve mental health is through the practice of gratitude. By focusing on what we are thankful for and by cultivating a sense of appreciation for the positive aspects of our lives, we can reduce stress and negative emotions, and improve our overall sense of well-being.

Finally, positive psychology can also play a role in improving mental health by promoting healthy relationships. By encouraging individuals to build positive relationships with others, and by teaching them the importance of effective communication and conflict resolution, positive psychology can help to reduce the risk of mental health problems and promote overall well-being.

In conclusion, positive psychology offers a number of strategies and techniques that can be used to improve mental health and promote well-being. Whether through promoting resilience, reducing symptoms of anxiety and depression, cultivating gratitude, or promoting healthy relationships, positive psychology can help individuals to lead happier, healthier, and more fulfilling lives.

21: Using Positive Thinking to Overcome Trauma

Trauma can have a profound and lasting impact on an individual's mental health, affecting their ability to lead a happy and fulfilling life. Positive thinking, however, has been shown to be a powerful tool for overcoming trauma and promoting recovery and healing.

One of the key ways in which positive thinking can be used to overcome trauma is by helping individuals to reframe negative experiences. By focusing on the positive aspects of a traumatic experience, and by looking for meaning and purpose in the experience, individuals can develop a more positive outlook on their traumatic experience and find hope and resilience in the face of adversity.

Another way in which positive thinking can help individuals to overcome trauma is by teaching them to practice mindfulness and meditation. These practices can help individuals to manage symptoms of anxiety and depression, reduce stress, and develop greater emotional regulation and resilience in the face of trauma.

In addition, positive thinking can help individuals to build

positive relationships and social support systems. By con-
necting with others who have experienced similar trauma,
individuals can find comfort, encouragement, and support,
and can develop a sense of community and belonging that
can be critical to their recovery and healing.

Another important aspect of using positive thinking to overcome trauma is learning to let go of negative thoughts and
emotions. By learning to identify and challenge negative
thoughts, and by replacing these thoughts with more positive and constructive thoughts, individuals can reduce symptoms of anxiety and depression and promote overall well-
being.

Finally, positive thinking can be used to overcome trauma
by promoting personal growth and self-discovery. By focusing on personal strengths and positive experiences, and by
developing a sense of purpose and meaning in life, individuals can find the resilience and inner strength they need to
overcome trauma and build a happier, healthier, and more
fulfilling life.

In conclusion, positive thinking is a powerful tool that can
be used to overcome trauma and promote recovery and

healing. Whether through reframing negative experiences, practicing mindfulness and meditation, building positive relationships, letting go of negative thoughts and emotions, or promoting personal growth and self-discovery, positive thinking can help individuals to lead happier, healthier, and more fulfilling lives in the aftermath of trauma.

22: The Positive Effects of Forgiveness

Forgiveness is a key aspect of positive psychology that has been shown to have numerous positive effects on mental and emotional health. By choosing to forgive others, individuals can free themselves from the negative emotions and stress associated with anger, resentment, and bitterness, and promote healing and well-being in their lives.

One of the key benefits of forgiveness is that it helps individuals to reduce stress and anxiety. When individuals hold on to anger and resentment towards others, they often experience high levels of stress, which can have negative impacts on their mental and physical health. By choosing to forgive, however, individuals can reduce stress and promote feelings of peace and calm in their lives.

Forgiveness also helps to promote positive relationships. When individuals forgive others, they often find that they are able to repair relationships that have been damaged by conflict or resentment, and develop stronger and more positive relationships with others. This can be particularly important in families and close relationships, where forgiveness can help to promote greater understanding, compassion, and support.

Another benefit of forgiveness is that it helps individuals to develop greater resilience and emotional regulation. By letting go of negative emotions such as anger and resentment, individuals can develop a greater capacity to manage stress and emotions, and can become more resilient in the face of life's challenges.

Forgiveness can also promote greater happiness and well-being. By releasing negative emotions, individuals can experience greater feelings of joy, peace, and contentment in their lives, and can develop a more positive outlook on life overall.

In conclusion, forgiveness is a key aspect of positive psychology that has numerous positive effects on mental and emotional health. Whether through reducing stress and anxiety, promoting positive relationships, developing greater resilience and emotional regulation, or promoting happiness and well-being, forgiveness can be a powerful tool for individuals looking to lead happier, healthier, and more fulfilling lives.

23: The Importance of Positive Social Support

Positive social support is an essential component of a happy and fulfilling life, and can have a profound impact on our mental, emotional, and physical well-being. Having supportive friends and family members can provide us with a sense of connection and belonging, and can help us to cope with life's challenges more effectively.

One of the key benefits of positive social support is that it helps to reduce stress and anxiety. When individuals have supportive friends and family members, they often experience lower levels of stress, as they know that they have people who care for them and are there for them in times of need. This can be especially important during difficult times, such as when individuals are facing major life changes, health problems, or other stressors.

Positive social support can also help to promote positive emotions, such as happiness, contentment, and joy. When individuals have supportive friends and family members, they often experience greater feelings of happiness and well-being, and can develop a more positive outlook on life overall.

Another benefit of positive social support is that it can help individuals to develop greater resilience and coping skills. When individuals have supportive friends and family members, they can turn to them for help and guidance during difficult times, and can receive the emotional support they need to help them cope with life's challenges more effectively.

Positive social support can also help individuals to develop stronger relationships with others. By having supportive friends and family members, individuals can form strong bonds with others and can feel a sense of connection and belonging in their relationships. This can be especially important for individuals who may feel lonely or isolated, as having positive social support can help to counteract these feelings and promote greater happiness and well-being.

In conclusion, positive social support is a critical aspect of a happy and fulfilling life, and can have numerous positive effects on our mental, emotional, and physical well-being. Whether through reducing stress and anxiety, promoting positive emotions, developing greater resilience and coping skills, or strengthening relationships with others, positive social support can help individuals to lead happier, healthier, and more fulfilling lives.

24: Positive Thinking and Spiritual Well-Being

Spiritual well-being refers to a sense of connection to something greater than oneself, a feeling of purpose and meaning in life, and a belief in a higher power. Positive thinking can play a significant role in enhancing spiritual well-being, as it can help individuals cultivate a deeper connection with their spirituality and find peace and fulfillment in their lives.

Studies have shown that people who have a positive outlook on life and practice positive thinking are more likely to have a stronger spiritual connection and a greater sense of purpose. This can be attributed to the fact that positive thinking can help individuals focus on the present moment and appreciate the beauty and wonder of the world around them. It also helps them to see the positive aspects of their lives and experience a greater sense of gratitude and contentment.

Moreover, positive thinking can help individuals overcome negative thoughts and emotions that may interfere with their spiritual well-being. By focusing on the positive aspects of life and looking for the good in difficult situations, individuals can better cope with stress and adversity, and maintain a sense of peace and serenity.

Positive thinking can also help individuals develop a deeper sense of compassion and empathy, which can enhance their spiritual well-being by allowing them to connect with others on a deeper level. This can lead to greater feelings of inter-connectedness and a stronger sense of community, which can further strengthen spiritual well-being.

In conclusion, positive thinking can play a vital role in en-hancing spiritual well-being. By cultivating a positive out-look on life, focusing on the present moment, and develop-ing a deeper connection with others, individuals can find greater meaning, purpose, and peace in their lives. To achieve greater spiritual well-being, it is important to prac-tice positive thinking regularly and make it a part of your daily routine.

25: The Benefits of Positive Thinking for Relationships

Positive thinking can have a profound impact on personal relationships and can play a significant role in enhancing the quality of these relationships. Positive thinking can help individuals view their relationships in a more positive light and focus on the positive aspects of their interactions with others. This can lead to greater happiness, satisfaction, and fulfillment in relationships.

One of the key benefits of positive thinking in relationships is improved communication. When individuals are in a positive state of mind, they are more likely to approach interactions with others in a more open and respectful manner. This can help to build trust and improve the overall quality of communication in relationships. Moreover, positive thinking can help individuals better understand and empathize with others, which can lead to more effective conflict resolution and a deeper sense of connection in relationships.

Positive thinking can also enhance the emotional intimacy in relationships by promoting positive emotions such as happiness, love, and gratitude. When individuals are in a positive state of mind, they are more likely to express their emotions and affection towards others, which can deepen emotional intimacy in relationships.

In addition, positive thinking can help individuals better navigate difficult situations in relationships. By focusing on the positive aspects of their interactions with others, individuals can maintain a sense of peace and stability, even in the face of adversity. This can help to reduce stress and improve the overall quality of relationships.

Finally, positive thinking can play a significant role in enhancing the longevity of relationships. By promoting positive emotions and a sense of fulfillment in relationships, individuals are less likely to experience feelings of boredom or dissatisfaction, which can contribute to the breakdown of relationships.

In conclusion, positive thinking can have a profound impact on personal relationships and can help individuals achieve greater happiness, satisfaction, and fulfillment in their interactions with others. To reap the benefits of positive thinking in relationships, it is important to make it a part of your daily routine and to focus on the positive aspects of your interactions with others.

26: The Benefits of Positive Thinking for Mental Health

Mental health is a crucial aspect of overall well-being and can greatly impact an individual's daily life. Positive thinking, a cornerstone of positive psychology, has been found to have significant benefits for mental health. In this chapter, we will explore the ways in which positive thinking can help improve mental health and promote well-being.

First and foremost, positive thinking can help reduce the negative impact of stress and anxiety. By focusing on the positive aspects of a situation, individuals can shift their perspective and better cope with stressful or anxious thoughts. This can lead to lower levels of anxiety and a more relaxed state of mind.

In addition, positive thinking can also help boost mood and counteract depression. When individuals focus on positive experiences and emotions, they can experience increased feelings of happiness and joy. This can help counteract feelings of sadness and hopelessness, which are common symptoms of depression.

Another way in which positive thinking can benefit mental

health is by improving self-esteem and confidence. When individuals adopt a positive outlook on life, they tend to feel more confident and capable. This, in turn, can help build resilience and reduce feelings of insecurity.

Furthermore, positive thinking can also help individuals develop a more optimistic outlook on life. When individuals focus on the positive, they are more likely to see challenges as opportunities for growth, rather than as insurmountable obstacles. This can lead to a more optimistic outlook on life, which can help boost overall well-being.

In conclusion, positive thinking has numerous benefits for mental health. By focusing on the positive aspects of life, individuals can reduce stress and anxiety, boost mood and counteract depression, improve self-esteem and confidence, and develop a more optimistic outlook on life. By incorporating positive thinking into your daily life, you can take a proactive approach to promoting your mental health and well-being.

27: Creating a Positive Home Environment

Your home is a sanctuary where you should feel safe, secure, and happy. However, for many people, the environment at home is not always positive and can contribute to feelings of stress and unhappiness. In this chapter, we will explore the importance of creating a positive home environment and how to achieve this through simple yet effective methods.

Positive environment = Positive Mood

Research has shown that the physical environment in which we live has a significant impact on our mood and overall well-being. A cluttered, chaotic, or gloomy environment can contribute to feelings of stress, anxiety, and depression, while a clean, organized, and well-lit environment can boost feelings of happiness and calmness.

Start with a Clean Home

Cleaning and decluttering your home is an excellent first step towards creating a positive environment. Start by getting rid of anything you no longer need or want. You can donate, sell, or recycle these items. Organize your home by creating systems that work for you and your family, such as designated storage spaces for items like toys, books, and clothes.

Incorporate Nature and Greenery

Nature has a positive effect on our mental and physical well-being, and incorporating plants and other natural elements into your home can enhance this effect. Research has shown that viewing greenery and natural environments can reduce stress, anxiety, and depression, and can boost feelings of happiness and well-being. Consider adding a few plants to your home, such as a potted herb, a fern, or a small flower arrangement.

Lighting Matters

Lighting is crucial in creating a positive home environment. Bright, natural light has been shown to boost feelings of happiness and well-being, while dim or artificial light can contribute to feelings of stress, anxiety, and depression. If possible, let natural light into your home by opening windows or adding skylights. If this is not an option, use bright and natural-looking artificial lights in your home, such as

LED or CFL bulbs.

Personalize Your Home

Your home should reflect your personal style and values. Adding personal touches to your home, such as family photos, artwork, and keepsakes, can create a sense of comfort and happiness. Consider creating a gallery wall of your favorite photos or artwork, or adding a personal touch to your furniture or decor by incorporating colors, patterns, or textures that you love.

In conclusion, creating a positive home environment is essential for your overall well-being. By decluttering, incorporating nature, using appropriate lighting, and personalizing your home, you can create a sanctuary that promotes happiness, comfort, and peace of mind. Remember that it is a gradual process and takes time, but the benefits are well worth the effort.

28: Positive Thinking for Athletes and Sports Performance

Athletic performance is not just about physical strength and ability, it also involves mental and emotional preparation. Positive thinking plays a crucial role in enhancing sports performance and can lead to increased confidence, motivation, and resilience.

The power of positive thinking in sports can be seen in the way athletes approach their training and competition. Athletes who adopt a positive mindset tend to have a more optimistic outlook and believe in their ability to succeed. This belief translates into higher levels of motivation, which in turn leads to better performance.

In addition, positive thinking can help athletes to manage their emotions during competition. It allows them to stay calm and focused even under pressure, which is crucial in high-stakes competitions. It also helps to reduce the impact of negative thoughts and emotions, such as fear, anxiety, and frustration, which can hinder performance.

One effective way to cultivate positive thinking in sports is to use affirmations and visualization techniques. Affirmations help to reinforce positive beliefs and attitudes, while visualization helps athletes to focus their thoughts on successful outcomes. For example, an athlete might visualize themselves crossing the finish line in first place, or hitting a game-winning shot.

Another way to enhance positive thinking in sports is to focus on the process rather than the outcome. This means focusing on things within the athlete's control, such as effort and technique, rather than external factors, such as winning or losing. This helps to reduce pressure and anxiety, allowing the athlete to perform to the best of their ability.

In addition to the benefits for individual athletes, positive thinking can also have a positive impact on team dynamics. Teams with positive attitudes and a strong sense of unity tend to perform better and have better outcomes than those without these qualities.

In conclusion, positive thinking is a powerful tool for enhancing sports performance. By developing a positive mindset, athletes can increase their confidence, motivation, and resilience, and overcome negative thoughts and emotions that may hinder their performance. With practice and persistence, athletes can cultivate a positive outlook that will serve them well both on and off the field.

29: Using Positive Thinking for Stress Management

Stress is an inevitable part of life, and it can take a toll on our physical and mental health if left unchecked. However, positive thinking can play a crucial role in managing stress and reducing its negative impact on our lives. In this chapter, we will explore the ways in which positive thinking can help us manage stress and lead to a happier, healthier life.

Positive Thinking and Stress Reduction

Research has shown that people who have a positive outlook on life experience lower levels of stress and anxiety than those who have a negative perspective. When we approach stress with a positive attitude, we are more likely to find solutions to problems and cope with stressful situations in a healthy and effective manner.

Positive self-talk is an essential tool for managing stress. When we encounter a stressful situation, our thoughts can spiral out of control and increase our levels of anxiety. However, by using positive self-talk, we can counteract these negative thoughts and calm our minds. This can involve reminding ourselves of past successes, focusing on the present moment, and using positive affirmations.

Mindfulness and Meditation

Mindfulness and meditation are powerful tools for managing stress. By becoming more aware of our thoughts and emotions, we can learn to control them and reduce stress levels. Mindfulness and meditation can help us focus on the present moment and reduce the negative impact of stress on our lives.

Setting Realistic Goals

Stress often arises when we feel overwhelmed by our responsibilities and the demands placed on us. Setting realistic goals can help us reduce stress levels by breaking down large tasks into manageable steps. This can involve prioritizing tasks, delegating responsibilities, and seeking help when needed.

Exercise and Physical Activity

Exercise and physical activity can help reduce stress levels and improve our overall mental health. Exercise releases endorphins, which are natural mood-boosters, and can help us feel more relaxed and calm. Regular physical activity can also help reduce anxiety, improve our mood, and increase our sense of well-being.

The Benefits of Positive Thinking for Stress Management

Positive thinking can help us manage stress and lead to a happier, healthier life. By using positive self-talk, mindfulness and meditation, setting realistic goals, and incorporating exercise into our daily routine, we can reduce stress levels and improve our overall mental health. Positive thinking allows us to approach stress in a proactive and productive manner, which can ultimately lead to a more fulfilling and satisfying life.

30: Positive Thinking for Career Success

Having a positive mindset can have a significant impact on your career success. Positive thinking can help you approach challenges with confidence, maintain a growth mindset, and increase your overall job satisfaction. In this chapter, we'll explore the connection between positive thinking and career success and how you can use positive psychology techniques to enhance your work life.

Confidence and a Growth Mindset

Confidence is a key factor in career success, and positive thinking can help build your self-assurance. When you focus on your strengths and acknowledge your successes, you can increase your confidence and approach challenges with a more positive outlook. Positive thinking also promotes a growth mindset, which is the belief that your abilities and intelligence can be developed through effort and dedication. This mindset allows you to tackle new tasks with eagerness and enthusiasm, rather than fear or avoidance.

Increased Job Satisfaction

Positive thinking can also lead to increased job satisfaction. When you approach your work with a positive attitude, you're more likely to find fulfillment and enjoyment in your daily tasks. This, in turn, can lead to higher motivation, increased productivity, and a greater sense of purpose in your work. Additionally, a positive work environment can help to reduce stress and improve your overall well-being, leading to a more positive and fulfilling career experience.

Positive Psychology Techniques for Career Success

There are several positive psychology techniques that you can use to enhance your career success. For example:

– Gratitude: Start each day by acknowledging the things you're grateful for, including your job and coworkers. This will help you maintain a positive attitude and improve your relationships with others.

– Positive self-talk: Reframe negative thoughts about your abilities and job into positive affirmations. For example, instead of thinking "I can't handle this task," think "I am capable and confident in my abilities."

– Mindfulness: Practice mindfulness in the workplace to reduce stress and increase focus. This can help you approach tasks with a clear mind and positive outlook.

– Setting and achieving positive goals: Set achievable goals for your career and use positive thinking to achieve them. Celebrate your successes and learn from your setbacks.

– Embracing positive emotions: Focus on experiencing positive emotions such as joy, contentment, and excitement in the workplace. This can help you approach work with a more positive and energetic outlook.

In conclusion, positive thinking is a powerful tool that can significantly enhance your career success. By incorporating positive psychology techniques into your work life, you can increase your confidence, job satisfaction, and overall well-being, leading to a happier and more fulfilling career experience.

31: Positive Thinking for Financial Success

Financial success is an important aspect of life, and positive thinking can play a significant role in achieving it. Positive thinking helps you maintain a healthy outlook on money and enables you to make better financial decisions. This chapter will explore the relationship between positive thinking and financial success, and provide you with strategies to cultivate a positive mindset in your financial life.

The first step towards financial success is to adopt a positive attitude towards money. This means that you need to view money as a tool that can help you achieve your goals and live a happy life, rather than as a source of stress and worry. When you adopt a positive mindset, you will find that it becomes easier to manage your finances and make smart financial decisions.

One of the key benefits of positive thinking for financial success is that it helps you to set realistic and achievable financial goals. When you approach financial planning from a positive perspective, you will be able to see the big picture, and you will be able to set goals that are aligned with your values and priorities. You will also be more motivated to work towards your goals, as you will see them as opportunities to improve your financial situation, rather than as obstacles to overcome.

In order to cultivate a positive mindset when it comes to money, it is important to focus on what you have, rather than what you don't have. This means that you need to be grateful for the financial resources that you have, and you need to recognize the value of your hard-earned money. When you focus on the positive aspects of your financial situation, you will be more likely to feel satisfied and content, and you will be less likely to fall into the trap of comparing yourself to others.

Another way to cultivate a positive mindset towards money is to practice positive affirmations. Positive affirmations are simple statements that you can repeat to yourself in order to reinforce positive beliefs about your finances. For example, you might repeat affirmations such as "I am worthy of financial success" or "I have the power to create financial abundance." When you repeat these affirmations on a regular basis, you will be able to develop a more positive outlook on money, and you will be more likely to achieve your financial goals.

Finally, it is important to remember that financial success is not just about having a lot of money. It is also about having peace of mind and feeling fulfilled in your financial life. When you adopt a positive mindset towards money, you will be able to find balance and enjoy the fruits of your financial success. You will also be better equipped to handle any financial setbacks that may arise, as you will have a resilient and positive attitude that will help you to bounce back quickly.

In conclusion, positive thinking can play a crucial role in financial success. By cultivating a positive mindset, setting realistic goals, focusing on what you have, practicing positive affirmations, and remembering the importance of balance and fulfillment, you will be able to unlock the power of positive thinking in your financial life, and achieve the financial success that you deserve.

32: The Benefits of Positive Thinking for Learning and Education

The power of positive thinking can have a profound impact on our lives, including in the realm of education and learning. A positive mindset can help us overcome obstacles, stay motivated, and increase our chances of success in both personal and professional development. In this chapter, we will explore the benefits of positive thinking for learning and education, and provide tips and techniques to help you apply these principles in your own life.

One of the main benefits of positive thinking for education is the impact it can have on motivation and persistence. When we approach our studies with a positive attitude, we are more likely to stick with the material, even when it becomes difficult. Positive self-talk and affirmations can help us to believe in ourselves and maintain a growth mindset, which is the belief that our abilities can be developed through effort and dedication.

Positive thinking can also help us to manage stress and anxiety, which are common challenges faced by students. By focusing on the present moment and cultivating gratitude, we can reduce stress and improve our overall well-being.

This can lead to improved focus and concentration, which are essential for success in the classroom.

Another benefit of positive thinking for education is the impact it can have on our relationships with teachers, classmates, and mentors. When we approach these relationships with a positive attitude, we are more likely to receive support and guidance, and to form strong bonds with others. This can lead to a more supportive and collaborative learning environment, which can be critical for success.

Positive thinking can also help us to develop critical thinking and problem-solving skills. By focusing on solutions rather than problems, we can approach challenges with a creative and innovative mindset, which can lead to breakthroughs and new insights. This can be particularly important for subjects like mathematics, science, and engineering, where problem-solving is a key component of success.

In conclusion, the benefits of positive thinking for learning and education are many and far-reaching. Whether you are a student, a teacher, or simply someone who is looking to improve their educational prospects, positive thinking can be a powerful tool to help you reach your goals. By incor-

porating positive thinking into your daily routine and making a conscious effort to stay focused on the positive, you
can unlock your full potential and take your education to
the next level.

33: Positive Thinking and Positive Aging

As people age, they may face a variety of challenges that can affect their mental and emotional well-being. These challenges may include physical health problems, retirement, the loss of loved ones, and decreased mobility. However, by embracing positive thinking and incorporating it into their daily lives, seniors can maintain and even improve their mental and emotional well-being as they age.

Positive thinking can help seniors maintain a positive outlook on life and age with grace, dignity, and joy. It can also help seniors overcome feelings of loneliness and isolation, improve their relationships with others, and foster a sense of purpose and meaning in their lives. Furthermore, positive thinking can help seniors to remain physically and mentally active, and may even help to improve their physical health.

One of the key benefits of positive thinking for seniors is its ability to help them to focus on their strengths and abilities, rather than their limitations. This focus on strengths and abilities can help seniors to remain engaged in their lives and feel a sense of purpose, even as they face new challenges. Additionally, positive thinking can help seniors to develop a sense of gratitude for what they have, and to appreciate each day as a gift.

Moreover, positive thinking can help seniors to overcome feelings of stress and anxiety, and to maintain a sense of resilience in the face of life's challenges. This can be especially important for seniors who may be facing health issues, financial concerns, or other difficulties. By approaching these challenges with a positive mindset, seniors can remain optimistic and find the strength and resilience to overcome them.

Finally, positive thinking can help seniors to foster strong and meaningful relationships with others. Whether it is through volunteering, participating in community events, or simply spending time with family and friends, positive thinking can help seniors to build and maintain relationships that are supportive, fulfilling, and uplifting.

In conclusion, positive thinking is a valuable tool for seniors as they navigate the challenges of aging. By embracing positive thinking, seniors can maintain and even improve their mental and emotional well-being, and live life to the fullest.

34: Positive Thinking and Environmental Sustainability

In recent years, the world has become increasingly aware of the impact of human activities on the environment and the importance of preserving the planet for future generations. Positive psychology provides a unique perspective on the relationship between human well-being and environmental sustainability. This chapter will explore how positive thinking can contribute to a more sustainable future.

First, it is important to understand the role of human behavior in environmental sustainability. The choices that individuals make on a daily basis, such as what they buy, how they travel, and how they use energy, have a significant impact on the environment. Positive thinking can play a crucial role in encouraging people to make choices that are more environmentally friendly.

For example, individuals who have a positive outlook on life are more likely to be proactive and take steps to reduce their carbon footprint. They may choose to use public transportation instead of driving, recycle, and buy products that are made from sustainable materials. When people feel good about themselves and their place in the world, they are more likely to act in ways that are beneficial to the environment.

Another aspect of positive thinking that is relevant to environmental sustainability is the concept of mindfulness. Mindfulness is the practice of being present in the moment and paying attention to one's thoughts and feelings. This practice can help people to become more aware of their actions and the impact they have on the environment. For example, a person who is mindful may take a moment to think about the environmental impact of buying a certain product before making a purchase. This type of reflection can lead to more environmentally conscious decisions.

In addition, positive thinking can help individuals to become more resilient in the face of environmental challenges. Climate change is an issue that is affecting communities all over the world, and it can be difficult for people to feel hopeful about the future. However, individuals who practice positive thinking are better equipped to handle difficult situations and remain optimistic even in the face of adversity. This resilience can be especially important when dealing with environmental issues that are likely to become more pressing in the coming years.

Finally, positive thinking can play a role in encouraging people to work together to address environmental challenges. When people feel good about themselves and their relationships with others, they are more likely to collaborate and find solutions to problems. For example, positive thinking can help individuals to engage in environmental activism, such as participating in marches, signing petitions, and joining advocacy groups. When people work together towards a common goal, they can achieve more than they could on their own.

In conclusion, positive thinking has the potential to contribute significantly to environmental sustainability. By encouraging individuals to make environmentally friendly choices, promoting mindfulness, building resilience, and fostering collaboration, positive thinking can help create a more sustainable future for everyone. Whether you are an individual, a community leader, or a policy maker, there is no doubt that positive thinking can play a role in promoting environmental sustainability.

35: The Future of Positive Psychology

Positive psychology is a relatively new field, having only been recognized as a separate branch of psychology in the late 20th century. In its relatively short existence, positive psychology has made significant progress in understanding the science of human happiness and well-being. The field has expanded rapidly and has become an integral part of the broader field of psychology. As the field continues to grow and evolve, researchers and practitioners are exploring new ways to apply positive psychology to improve people's lives.

In the future, we can expect positive psychology to continue to play an important role in shaping our understanding of human happiness and well-being. Researchers are already exploring new topics such as the impact of positive thinking on physical health, the benefits of positive thinking for mental health, and the role of positive thinking in overcoming trauma. As technology continues to advance, we can expect positive psychology to utilize new tools and techniques to reach a wider audience and help people from all walks of life.

35: THE FUTURE OF POSITIVE PSYCHOLOGY

In addition, positive psychology is likely to continue to expand into new areas, such as education, career success, financial success, and environmental sustainability. This will provide opportunities for individuals, organizations, and communities to apply the principles of positive psychology in new and innovative ways.

In conclusion, the future of positive psychology looks bright and promising. As we continue to learn more about the benefits of positive thinking and positive emotions, we can expect positive psychology to play an increasingly important role in improving people's lives and creating a happier and more fulfilling world.

36: Conclusion: Embracing Positive Thinking for a Happier, Fulfilling Life

Positive psychology is a powerful tool that can help you transform your life and achieve happiness, success, and fulfillment. The techniques and strategies outlined in this book, such as gratitude, positive self-talk, mindfulness, goal setting, resilience building, and many others, are scientifically proven to improve your mental and physical health, boost your confidence and self-esteem, strengthen your relationships, and promote success in all areas of life.

By embracing positive thinking, you can overcome negative thoughts and emotions, reduce stress, improve your mental and physical health, and find purpose and meaning in life. Whether you're a student, a parent, an athlete, a professional, or just someone looking for a happier, more fulfilling life, positive psychology has something to offer you.

So what can you do to embrace positive thinking and start enjoying its many benefits? Here are a few tips to get you started:

– Start each day with positive affirmations. Repeat positive statements about yourself and your life to build confidence and self-esteem.

– Practice gratitude by keeping a gratitude journal. Write down three things you're grateful for each day.

– Surround yourself with positive people. Seek out friends and family members who are supportive and uplifting, and limit your time with negative or toxic individuals.

– Cultivate mindfulness through meditation or other relaxation techniques. Take time each day to focus on the present moment and cultivate inner peace and tranquility.

– Set achievable, positive goals for yourself and work towards them every day.

– Embrace positive emotions, such as joy, love, and contentment, and strive to experience them as often as possible.

By incorporating these techniques and strategies into your daily life, you can unlock the power of positive thinking and create a happier, more fulfilling life for yourself. Remember, positive psychology is not about ignoring life's challenges or difficulties, but about learning to approach them with a positive, optimistic mindset. When you embrace positive thinking, you'll be amazed at the positive impact it has on every aspect of your life. So why wait? Start embracing positive thinking today and unlock the power of a happier, more fulfilling life!

Thank You

As we reach the end of this book, I want to say thanks for reading this book.

I want to get this information out to as many people as possible. If you found this book helpful, I would greatly appreciate you leaving me a review. This helps others find the book as well.

Disclaimer

This document is geared towards providing exact and reliable information in regards to the topic and issue covered. The publication is sold on the idea that the publisher is not required to render an accounting, officially permitted, or otherwise, qualified services. If advice is necessary, legal, financial, medical or professional, a practiced individual in the profession should be ordered.

This information is not presented by a financial or medical practitioner and is for entertainment, educational and informational purposes only. The content is not intended as a substitute for professional medical advice, diagnosis, or treatment. Always seek the advice of your physician or other qualified health care provider with any questions you may have regarding a medical condition. Never disregard professional medical advice or delay in seeking it because of something you have read.

The information provided herein is stated to be truthful and consistent, in that any liability, in terms of inattention or otherwise, by any usage or abuse of any policies, processes, or directions contained within is the solitary and utter responsibility of the recipient reader. Under no circumstances

DISCLAIMER

will any legal responsibility or blame be held against the publisher for any reparation, damages, or monetary loss due to the information herein, either directly or indirectly.

www.ingramcontent.com/pod-product-compliance
Lightning Source LLC
Chambersburg PA
CBHW060333130626
46553CB00003B/1002